1 MONTH OF
FREE
READING

at
www.ForgottenBooks.com

By purchasing this book you are eligible for one month membership to ForgottenBooks.com, giving you unlimited access to our entire collection of over 1,000,000 titles via our web site and mobile apps.

To claim your free month visit: www.forgottenbooks.com/free987762

* Offer is valid for 45 days from date of purchase. Terms and conditions apply.

ISBN 978-0-260-92191-8
PIBN 10987762

This book is a reproduction of an important historical work. Forgotten Books uses state-of-the-art technology to digitally reconstruct the work, preserving the original format whilst repairing imperfections present in the aged copy. In rare cases, an imperfection in the original, such as a blemish or missing page, may be replicated in our edition. We do, however, repair the vast majority of imperfections successfully; any imperfections that remain are intentionally left to preserve the state of such historical works.

Forgotten Books is a registered trademark of FB &c Ltd.
Copyright © 2018 FB &c Ltd.
FB &c Ltd, Dalton House, 60 Windsor Avenue, London, SW19 2RR.
Company number 08720141. Registered in England and Wales.

For support please visit www.forgottenbooks.com

First Presbyterian Church
Brockville.

Historical Sketch, 1811-1900

Annual Reports
For Year Ending December 31, 1900.

REV. WM. SMART

F501

HISTORICAL SKETCH

OF THE FIRST PRESBYTERIAN CHURCH BROCKVILLE, ONT.

1811-1900

At the close of what is now termed the Revolutionary War, between Great Britain and her American Colonies, a number of professing Christians found their way to Canada, many of whom were connected with the Presbyterian Church. Several of these families settled in the vicinity of Brockville, within what was then known as the District of Johnstown.

In those early days, the securing of Gospel ordinances was a matter of great difficulty, churches there were none, and only occasionally did a minister of God find his way among the settlers. Indeed the late revered Adiel Sherwood stated that the only religious services engaged in for several years, were in attending a Masonic Lodge, which had been instituted and carried on under the auspices of officers of the regular army.

Religious exercises of this nature, however, did not satisfy the cravings of the people for a Gospel ministry, and it was decided to transmit a memorial to the General Assembly of the Church of Scotland, for spiritual aid. This memorial was sent through the Rev. John Bethune of Williamstown, but elicited no response. After a long period of waiting an appeal was made to the Associate Reformed Synod of the United States, through Dr. Mason of New York. This body took the matter into their serious consideration, but were unable to promise permanent relief. Travelling missionaries, however, were sent, and the Rev. Messrs Proudfoot, Goodwillie, Dunlop and others, did much to keep the Gospel flame alive among the scattered population of Upper Canada. But this was not deemed sufficient. A Gospel Ministry was desired, and being unsuccessful in their applications to the bodies already mentioned, a third memorial was prepared and forwarded to the Dutch Reformed Church of the United

States. Again they were disappointed. At length the people of Elizabethtown and Yonge united in a call to the Rev. Robert McDowell, who had been laboring for several years in the Bay of Quinte District. Here also they were doomed to disappointment, as Mr. McDowell decided to remain in Ernestown, although he frequently visited Johnstown District.

So many disappointments would have worn out the patience of less zealous and ardent adherents of the cause, but they were not thus daunted, and at last, through the counsel of Dr. Mason of New York, succeeded in securing aid through the London Missionary Society. The result was the settlement here of the Rev. William Smart, then a student in the Theological Seminary at Gosport. Though preparing to go as a Missionary to Calcutta, he was strongly urged and finally consented to change his plans, and accept the invitation to come to Elizabethtown. Mr. Smart was ordained a minister in Scot's Church, Swallow Street, London, April 11th, 1811, by Rev. Dr. Nichol, and soon afterwards sailed for Canada, arriving at Elizabethtown on Oct. 7th of the same year. Mr. Smart desired one year in which to consider whether he would settle permanently, and in event of this it was agreed that the sum of one hundred and fifty Pounds should be paid him annually, as he had no income from the London Missionary Society.

One of his first acts, in the very month in which he reached this field of labor, Oct. 1811, was the organization of the first Sabbath School in Canada, of which the late Adiel Sherwood was the first superintendent.

(Reproduced from a wood cut print taken when Mr. Smart was about 22 years of age, and sent to Brockville before Mr. Smart came to the country.)

Before this year of probation, already referred to, had expired, war was declared by the United States against Great Britain, and on the outbreak of hostilities, all became confusion throughout the country. Even at this critical time, God in his good providence, opened up a way for the settlement of Mr. Smart. A meeting was called, and a long document drawn up, and subscribed, in which the people of Elizabethtown, Yonge and Augusta became bound to raise by subscription a stipend of one hundred and fifty Pounds per annum. This document was dated Oct. Oct. 3rd, 1812, and was signed and sealed by the following, viz. :

James Breakenridge, Joseph McNish, Bartholomew Carley, Adiel Sherwood, Robert McLean, Archibald McLean, Peter Purvis, Elnathan Hubble, Josiah Jones, James Dunham, Rufus C. Henderson and William Wells.

Mr. Smart made Brockville the special sphere of his Sunday labors, and on week days visited and preached in regular order at the various settlements from Gananoque to Matilda, and from the front to Bathurst, and eventually to Perth.

Church organization was discussed, but not deemed expedient, on account of the unsettled state into which the war had thrown the country. Late in 1815 and early in 1816 the subject was again energetically taken up and several meetings held, at which the nature and design of a Christian Church was explained, and ultimately Tuesday, the 12th day of March, 1816, was set apart as a special day of prayer and fasting. During the exercises of this day another document was drawn up, containing certain rules for the guidance of the officers, in managing the spiritual and temporal affairs of the congregation, and was signed by the Minister and twenty-five others, as follows, viz:—

Peter Purvis, John McCready, James Gibson, David McCready, Catherine Purvis, Anna McCready, Allan Grant, Mrs. Grant, Alexander McLean, Sr., Jane McLean, Alexander McLean, Jr., Jane Taylor, Anna McLean, Henry McLean, Nancy McLean, Rebecca McLean, Nehemiah Seaman, Margaret Seaman, David McCready, Mary McCready, Sedate Jones, Philena Jones, Janet Morris, Margaret Simpson and Ann Fraser. These constituted the First Presbyterian Church of Brockville.

On Sunday following, March 17th, the following persons were ordained as elders, by the Rev. William Smart, in the Court House, Brockville, viz: Peter Purvis, John McCready, James Gibson and

David McCready, and after the ordination service the Sacrament of the Lord's Supper was dispensed.

The Communion was again held in July of the same year, when five other names were added to the roll of the church.

On Nov. 17th, 1816, Mr. Smart was married to Philena, widow of the late Israel Jones, by the Rev. John Bethune, first settled clergyman in connection with St. Peter's Anglican congregation of this town.

Mr. Smart was prominent in the work of organizing "The Presbytery of the Canadas" (Upper and Lower), on July 9th, 1818. At the first meeting only five ministers were present. Upper and Lower Canada at that date represented Ontario and Quebec. This was the first Presbytery organized in these two provinces.

At a meeting of session held on May 12th, 1819, it was decided to ask the Rev Robert McDowell of Ernestown and Rev. Robert Easton

of Montreal, to take part in the "opening exercises" of the church on Sunday, June 22nd next. As no further statement is made, it is inferred that the First Church building was dedicated on that date. Mr. Smart contributed one year's stipend to the building fund of this structure. The land upon which the building was erected was generously donated for that purpose by William Buell, Esq., one of the earliest settlers, and great-grandfather of W. S. Buell, Esq., Mayor of Brockville. The structure was of stone, with square tower, to which the steeple and a bell were afterwards added, as well as a gallery inside. The accompanying illustration has been pronounced an accurate representation, although the drawing was made partly by inference, from customs known to have existed in the days when the church was built, and partly (the roof and spire), from a drawing in the possession of G A. Dana, Esq., Sheriff.

The "Synod of the Canadas" was organized in 1820, and the First Church, through Mr. Peter Purvis, gave its adherence in 1821.

Rev. Mr. Smart visited Great Britain in 1825, and no meetings of session are recorded from Oct 1st, 1825, to Sept. 25th, 1826.

On April 12th, 1827, Messrs. John Dickey and Truelove Butler were ordained elders.

Mr. Smart took a decided stand against the "Clergy Reserves," and as Moderator of "The United Presbytery of Upper Canada" was instrumental in a petition being presented from that body to Parliament, praying for a change in the system of education. The result was not very gratifying. He was also active in missionary work, in which the matter of distance does not appear to have been of much consideration, as a prominent Q. C of Toronto states, "we met Mr. Smart in 1837, between Chatham and London, travelling on horseback, having his Bible and saddlebags, doing missionary work among the Indians about Thamesville and Deleware."

At a meeting of the United Presbytery of Upper Canada, held in First Church, June 17th, 1830, that body organized itself into the "United Synod of Upper Canada," having two Presbyteries, viz., Brockville with seven and York with eight ministers.

The decease of Mr. Truelove Butler and the licensing of Mr. John Dickey to preach, elders of this congregation, necessitated the enlargement of the session, when Messrs. George McNish and Alex. McLean were nominated to the office.

On July 3rd, 1840, the United Synod of Upper Canada, of which Mr. Smart was Moderator, and the Synod of the Church of Scotland were united as "The Synod of Canada." The congregation of First Church voted unanimously to adhere to the union thus formed, one stipulation only being made, "that the session shall not be considered as pledging itself to support or approve of patronage." On Nov. 4th, 1843, Mr. Smart notified the session that he had withdrawn from the Synod of Canada and was sustained by session and congregation both at Brockville and Yonge.

The last meeting of Session recorded in Mr. Smart's handwriting is under date of Dec. 30, 1843.

Dr. Burns, a deputy of the Free Church of Scotland, visited the Congregation on April 22, 1844, and delivered an address on the principles, progress and prospects of the Free Church, encouraging and confirming the congregation in the course they had lately taken.

The records of the congregation do not contain anything of sufficient importance to be recorded here, until Tuesday, January 12th 1847, on which date the first church edifice was burned. The fire originated at night and in the vicinity of the main entrance so that the bell (which was used as the town fire bell at that time) was very early in the progress of the fire loosened from its hangers and fell into the cellar. Consequently no alarm was given, and the building was totally destroyed. The congregation was then forced to occupy the stone school house on the rock at corner Perth and George streets (now used as a blacksmith shop) as a place of worship.

On Sunday, April 11th, 1847, the minister announced to his congregation that a meeting would be held on the morning of Monday to consider ways and means of providing a place of worship. The meeting was held, resolutions carried, and boards of trustees and management were appointed. That same afternoon a joint meeting of these two boards was held, and at the adjournment sub-committees had been appointed, and R. P. Colton had subscribed the brick to erect the church, which was forty by sixty feet, built of brick with cut stone front corners.

The chairmen of committees were as follows : Excavation and mason work, Alexander Starr ; supply of materials, R P. Colton, chairman ; superintendent of woodwork, John McElhenny.

On Sept. 27, 1847, Rev. Mr. Smart transferred the property, which he had received in trust from Wm. Buell, Esq., in accordance with the conditions of the original title deed, to the following, viz. : John McLean, and James Breakenridge, Elizabethtown ; George McNish, Yonge ; Robert Edmondson and Reuben Powers Colton, of Brockville, " Trustees in whose names the property should be held by the corporate name of the First Presbyterian Church of the Town of Brockville and their successors in office forever."

It was decided at a meeting of the Board of Management on Jan. 24, 1848, that it was expedient to provide an assistant for the Rev. Mr.

HISTORICAL SKETCH. 11

Smart, and on March 28th the same year, the Rev. John McMurray preached before the congregation and was present at meeting of session.

Mr. McMurray was of Seaton, Delaval, Newcastle-on-Tyne, England, and had been sent out by the Free Church of Scotland Home Mission Committee, and on July 19th, 1848, he was inducted as colleague and successor to Mr. Smart.

On Aug. 6, 1848, the new church was opened and dedicated, and at the same service the Lord's Supper was dispensed to sixty, who had been members before Mr. McMurray's arrival, thirty who had been since admitted and eleven who were admitted on that day for the first time, one hundred and one in all. Rev.

REV. JOHN McMURRAY.

Messrs. Smart and McMurray officiated. The church as opened on this date had no steeple, bell or gallery, and the basement had not been excavated. The latter was done during the summer of 1851, and the steeple and gallery were added later.

On Aug. 16th, 1848, the congregation met and nominated and elected elders and deacons, and on Oct. 4th the ordination took place. James Breakenridge, Dr. Robert Edmondson and James Johnston were set apart as ruling elders, and John McElhenny, John Anderson, John Moffatt, George Stuart, Samuel Logan and Wm. S. McCready as deacons. Mr. Smart resigned the charge of First Church on Feb. 6th, 1849, but continued to preach to the rural part of the congregation until about 1862, when his first wife having died in 1855, he married Mrs. Bush of Gananoque and removed there. Rev. Mr. Smart breathed his last at Gananoque on Sept. 9th, 1876, only five days less than 88 years of age.

REV. WM. SMART.

During the long and changing years of more than half a century's service devoted to those around him, without respect of persons, he never lost the esteem and respect which he secured at the start by his kindly and consistent Christian character, and his manifest faith in the truth that he preached.

. The remains were brought to Brockville by steamer on Tuesday, 15th, arriving here at 1.45 p. m., when a large number of our oldest citizens were in waiting to pay their last tribute of respect. The procession formed and wended its way to the First Presbyterian church, where a short service was held, and thence to the cemetery, where the remains were laid alongside of the partner of, and in the midst of the scenes of, his most active and useful labors. A neat monument marks the spot where lie his remains and those of his first wife, erected (by consent of the relatives), jointly by admirers in this section and the relatives of the deceased.

The minutes of a Congregational meeting held on March 17, 1852, Sheriff Adiel Sherwood in the chair, contain a brief statement of receipts and expenditure for the year previous. The receipts from pew rents were £138 1s. 4½d, and from plate collections £36 3s. 5d. ; total £174 4s. 9½d. Of this amount the minister had been paid £161, and £23 4s. 4½d expended for incidentals, leaving 5d. in the treasury.

The Deacons' Court organized on Oct. 4, 1848, was dissolved on Oct. 15, 1851, because it proved to be of little use, owing to the "Title Deed" under which the Church property was held.

Mr. McMurray handed in his resignation of the pastoral charge of the congregation at a meeting of Presbytery held at Ottawa on March 4, 1856.

REV. J. K. SMITH.

The Rev. J. K. Smith of Ramsay, met with the session on May 29th, 1856, probably preaching on that day, and was inducted into the charge of the congregation on Oct. 2nd. Mr Smith was born in Aberdeen, Scotland, on April 11, 1827, and studied successively in Marischall College, Aberdeen Free Church Divinity Hall and The Free Church College, Edinburgh, and was licensed to preach in 1851, by the Presbytery of Aberdeen. He came to Canada in the fall of the year and early in 1853 was inducted into the charge of the Presbyterian Church at Ramsay (now Almonte) and on Oct 2, 1856, into the First Church, Brockville. In making the call to Mr. Smith, the annual stipend was increased from £150 to £200, " in order to secure the services of an active zealous minister."

At a meeting of the trustees held on Feb. 23, 1857, a committee was appointed to obtain plans and specifications for a spire and gallery for the church. These improvements were completed during the year, the expense being stated as £466.

An incident of much concern to the congregation occurred about the end of the year 1860, when the treasurer of the Church Funds took a hasty visit to Ogdensburg, and did not come back. It does not appear, however, that the absconder had very much of the congregational funds with him, but this incident, together with the very disorderly way his records had been kept, caused not a little uncertainty and much inconvenience.

In that year also difficulties occurred over the introduction of an organ, as an aid to the musical services of the church. Considerable feeling was generated in the matter and even an edict of Synod was pigeon holed, but finally the organ was removed to the manse on June 22, 1862. Not very long afterwards the Synod decreed that organs might be used and the instrument was returned to its place in the gallery.

On Nov. 2nd, 1862, the Fairfield Mission was organized and while Mr. Smith remained in Brockville he carried on this work.

The session met on Jan. 27th, 1863, and purged the communion roll, when it was found that from 84 communicants at Mr. Smith's first communion service, the membership had increased to 191 members in the Brockville congregation and 35 at Fairfield Mission.

A Deacons' Court was again introduced on Feb. 10th, 1864, when James Raphael, Thomas King, James Nicholl, R. Bryson and Thomas Wilkinson were ordained as such.

At the expressed desire of the Fairfield congregation the following elders were ordained on Feb. 16th, 1865. James Cowan, J. W. Hough, Henry Quartus, Walsingham Moore, William Allan and David McCracken.

Dr. Edmondson, Sheriff Sherwood, Thomas King and J. R. Roper were elected representatives of the congregation to attend Presbytery meeting at Prescott, 28th Sept., 1865, but were not able to prevent Rev. Mr. Smith's resignation of this congregation being accepted by that body. On their return a purse of $700 was raised in three hours as a last effort to induce Mr. Smith to remain (it being intended to add that amount to his stipend for the current year), but without avail, and Mr. Smith was inducted into the charge of Knox Church, Galt, on Oct. 5th, 1865. We shall make room for a verse or two from the then Poet Laureate of Canadian Journalists, the late Col. David Wylie, written on this occasion:

>"The teacher smiled, and an angel said,
>   Go forth to thy work again,
>It is not in vain that the seed is shed,
>If only one soul to the cross is led,
>   "Thy labor is not in vain."

>"Then rise, fellow teacher, to labor go,
>   Wide scatter the precious grain,
>Though the fruit may never be seen below,
>Be sure that the seed of the word will grow,
>Toil on in faith, and thou shalt know,
>   "Thy labor is not in vain."

Rev. J. K. Smith at present resides in Toronto, having laid aside the activities of a settled charge. Since leaving Brockville he has occupied important charges at Galt, San Francisco, Halifax, N. S., London, Eng., and from 1892 to 1898 was pastor of First Church, Port Hope. In 1886 the Montreal College conferred on Mr. Smith the degree of Doctor of Divinity, and he was elected Moderator of the General Assembly in the same year.

The Rev. John Jones, whose portrait is here inserted, was called by the congregation by Feb. 7th, 1866, and was inducted into the charge on the 25th of the following May. Mr. Jones was born at Llanerchymeed, Anglesey, Wales, in March, 1835, came to America in 1854, and graduated from Princeton College in 1865. He was called to Cote des Neiges, Montreal, the same year and to Brockville in the year following.

During Mr. Jones' short ministry the membership of the session was increased, Alex. G. McCready, Dr. Gordon and Robert Graham being ordained on Jan. 15th, 1868.

REV. JOHN JONES.

On Sept. 9th, 1869, Mr. Jones resigned the charge of First Church, intending to make an extended trip to Europe and the Holy Land. Rev. Mr. Jones is still residing in Montreal and has been largely instrumental in building up the Mile End Mission (now Chalmers Church), and the congregation of Taylor Church. His labors in both of these charges were practically without remuneration.

The Rev. Albert Jones Traver, M. A., the next minister, was inducted over the congregation on Aug. 25th, 1870. The Rev. Messrs. Burton of Prescott, Mackenzie (father of Rev. W. A. Mackenzie), of South Gower, and Bennett of Kemptville, officiating. Mr. Traver was born in Trenton, Jan. 26th, 1840, educated at Toronto University, and graduated with high honors, when he was called to Berlin, Ont., and thence to Brockville.

REV. ALBERT JONES TRAVER.

The session was increased during Mr. Traver's ministry by the addition of Messrs. James Raphael, Henry Freeland and John M. Gill on May 3rd, 1874.

Mr. Traver's ministry was of less than five years' duration, when, after an illness covering some months, he fell asleep on Thursday, August 5th, 1875. The remains were taken for interment to Trenton, the residence of his parents. As an evidence of consecrated life and its influence, it is only necessary to state that the membership was increased from 130 to 260 during this short ministry.

On March 16th, 1876, a call was extended to the Rev. Geo. Burnfield, M. A., of Scarborough, which resulted in Mr. Burnfield being inducted over the congregation on April 27th. Mr. Burnfield had not been in Brockville more than a year and a half when it became evident that the church building then used was not going to accommodate the congregation very long. From November 22nd, 1877, to Feb. 6th, 1878, several meetings were held, resulting at the last date, in a report stating that $16,410 had been subscribed towards a new building, and finance and building committees were appointed. The finance committee consisted of James Moore, Robert Gill, John F. Wood, W. H. Comstock, G. W. McCullough and Thos. Gilmour; building committee, John M. Gill, Thomas Wilkinson, Newton Cossitt, Sr., Wm. Gilmour, Wm. McCullough, John Lafayette and W. R. Bell.

The first step towards tearing down the church was the removal of the pews from the center aisle during the day, and a "farewell social," was held in the evening on Monday, May 28th, 1878, when, as a final number on the programme, the late Col. Wylie read an historical sketch of the church and congregation since its inception in 1811, and also a poem dedicated to the "Old church," and entitled "A Farewell Ode."

REV. GEO. BURNFIELD.

FAREWELL ODE TO THE OLD CHURCH.

Farewell old temple, soon thy walls must fall,
  Which oft resounded to the Gospel call,
Farewell old pews, farewell old pulpit, too,
  Thy day is served, we yearn for something new ;
And yet, when thou art gone and seen no more,
  Will souls be fed from better Gospel store ?
God grant it may be so, and that to Heaven
  Many true doers of the word be given.

Thy form, old temple, may not please the eye,
  Thy twisted steeple, pointing to the sky,
May mar thy beauty in the critic's mind,
  Who find more grace in the M. E.'s behind.

Thy cellar basement, too, with dark damp floor,
  With those no longer can we feel secure,
And, to sum up, thy limit's too confined,
  To be in keeping with the march of mind.

And yet, with all thy quaintness, all thy ill,
  Old church, "With all thy faults we love thee still."

There from that pew, the loving father's gone,
  To join the ransomed throngs around the throne,
There from that seat, the mother good and pure,
  Who laid her faith on Christ, foundation sure,
On wings of love and with her soul elate,
  Has reached her home above, through pearly gate,
Some to that font were brought in swaddlings bound,
  Baptismal entrance to the Church thus found.

There daughter, son, brother and sister, too,
  Have "Gone before," from that old family pew,
Have reached the "Church not made with hands," above,
  And bask in bliss, all through a Saviour's love.
Yes, good old temple, hallowed memories will
  Wreathe themselves round our hearts when thou art still.

Some may remember their first earnest prayer;
  That in Christ's sacrifice they too might share,
Some pointed sermon in the ear may ring,
  And to the heart sweet consolation bring,
That seed was planted there in faith and love,
  To bring fruition in the Church above.

And now, old temple, we must part at last,
  Thy days are numbered—all thy glories past;
How hard to say—oh, who can truly tell
  The anguish in the words—A Long Farewell.

The present edifice was dedicated on Sunday, Dec 14, 1879, having been erected at a cost of $35,000.00. Rev. Dr. McVicar, of Montreal; Rev. J. K. Smith, of Port Hope, and Rev. Dr. Grant, of Kingston, presided at the morning, afternoon and evening services respectively. About

$650.00 were realized from the collections of the day, and this was increased to $750.00 at the social on the following evening. On Oct. 5th, 1881, an election of elders took place resulting in P. C. McGregor, James Lanskail and Newton Cossitt being elected. These were ordained on 21st of the same month.

Mr. Burnfield visited the Holy Land during his pastorate here, leaving on Nov. 16th, 1881, and returning on June, 7th, 1882. At a meeting of Presbytery held at Prescott, Dec 6th, 1887, Mr. Burnfield resigned the pastoral charge of the congregation. Mr. Burnfield removed to Toronto and after a short pastorate in South side Church, became pastor of North Presbyterian Church of Philadelphia, Penn., the Scots Kirk of that city.

WM. A. McKENZIE, B.A., B.D.

Rev. Wm. A. McKenzie, B.A., B.D., was inducted into the pastoral charge of the congregation on Tuesday, July 26th, 1888, Rev. Messrs. McWilliams, Alex. McGillivray, Geo. Macarthur and D. Y. Ross officiating. Mr. McKenzie was born at Barrie, Ont., in Oct., 1855, educated in Upper Canada and McGill College, and graduated from the Presbyterian College, Montreal, as a gold medalist in Theology. He served one year as a Missionary in the North-West, three years at Grafton, Ont., and from that place was called to Brockville.

On May 19, 1889, Messrs. John R. Reid, Allan Cameron, Robert Graham and Robert Grant were ordained to the eldership of the Church.

During the summer of 1894 extensive alterations and improvements to the extent of $7,500 were made in the church building. The reopening, was introduced by a very elaborate organ recital on Thursday evening, Oct. 31st, and special services the following Sunday, Nov. 3rd, conducted in the morning and evening by Dr. G. M. Grant, of Queen's, Kingston, and in the afternoon by Dr. Grant and the local clergymen of the town.

Mr. Mackenzie resigned his pastorate of the congregation at Prescott on Oct. 5, 1898, and since then had an important charge at Ottumwa, Ill., and is at present in New York city. The Presbyterian College, of

Montreal, conferred the degree of Doctor of Divinity on Mr. Mackenzie in 1899.

On July 3rd, 1899, the congregation, without a dissenting voice, united in a call to the Rev. Robert Laird, M. A., then of Campbellford, without a bearing, on the report of Sheriff G. A. Dana, Capt. Buckman and Mr. Robert Laidlaw. Mr. Laird was born at Malpeque, P. E. I., is a graduate of Queen's College, Kingston, a gold medalist in classics. After graduating in 1895, he was called to Campbellford Church, and in 1897 took a post graduate course at Berlin, Germany, In April, 1898, Mr. Laird was married to Miss Odell of Belmont, Ont., also a graduate of Queens. After a four years' pastorate at Campbellford, Mr. Laird was translated into First Church, Brockville, on Sept. 6th, 1899, the Rev. Messrs. J. J. Cameron, Athens; George Macarthur, Cardinal; E. S. Logie, Winchester, and D. Strachan of St. John's Church officiating at the induction services.

REV ROBERT LAIRD, M. A.

The closing year of the century was marked by two noteworthy items of history. The sum of $7,000 was paid on the church debt, and changes have been made in the regulations of the Trust Deeds under which the church property is held, bringing them into uniformity with the rules of procedure and practice of the Presbyterian Church in Canada.

The membership on Dec. 31st, 1900, is 403 and the outlook is promising.

CHURCH SESSION.

MINISTER.

Rev. Robert Laird, M.A.

ELDERS.

Newton Cossitt, Sr.,   John M. Gill, (Clerk),   Robt. Grant,

Allan Cameron,   James Lanskail.

BOARD OF MANAGERS.

Thos. Wilkinson,   Robt. Laidlaw,

Chairman and Treas.   Rec.-Sec'y.

J. T. Tennant, Financial Secretary.

John Menish,   H. S. Seaman.

TRUSTEES OF CHURCH PROPERTY.

Thos. Wilkinson,   J. T. Tennant,   John Menish,

H. S. Seaman,   Robt. Laidlaw.

CHOIR.

Conductor—F. H. Fulford.

Organist—Miss M. Abbott.

GENERAL ANNOUNCEMENTS.

Public Worship, Sabbath, - - - 11 a.m. and 7 p.m.
Sabbath School and Bible Class, - - - - 2:45 p.m.

The Weekly Prayer Meeting is held on Wednesday evening at 8 o'clock, in the Lecture Room.

The Teachers of the Sabbath School meet every Wednesday evening before the prayer meeting.

The Y. P. S. C. E. meets every Sunday evening at 6:10 o'clock.

The Junior Y. P. S. C. E. meets every Sunday morning at 10:10.

The Woman's Foreign Missionary Society meets in the ladies' parlor of the Church the first Thursday in each month at 3 p. m.

The Young Ladies' Mission Band meets on the second Thursday in each month at 8 p. m.

Applications for Sittings are made to the Committee of Managers, Messrs. J. T. Tennant and H. S. Seaman.

The church is supported by voluntary contributions. Envelopes for these may be had on application to the Financial Secretary.

The Sacrament of Baptism is administered on application being made to the minister.

The Sacrament of the Lord's Supper is observed on the first Sabbath of March, June, September and December.

CONGREGATIONAL MEETINGS.

The annual meeting of the male members of the congregation was held in accordance with the title deed of the church on Monday, Jan. 1, 1900, to elect trustees for the year.

Rev. R. Laird was in the the chair and R. Laidlaw was appointed Secretary.

A resolution was passed appointing the following trustees of the church and manse property for the ensuing year: Thomas Wilkinson, J. T. Tennant, John Menish, H. S. Seaman and R. Laidlaw.

The annual meeting of the congregation was held on Jan. 24, 1900.

After a short service of prayer and praise the meeting was organized with the pastor, Rev. Robert Laird in the chair and Robert Laidlaw, Secretary.

The minutes of the congregational meetings held during the year 1899 were confirmed.

The reports for the year 1900 of the session, Board of Trustees, Treasurer, Financial Secretary, Sabbath School, Senior and Junior Y. P. S. C E, Woman's Foreign Missionary Society, Young Ladies' Mission Band, Treasurer of Relief Fund, etc., were received and on motion adopted.

Resolutions were passed appointing the following church officers for the current year:

Plate Collectors—Wm. Sutherland, R. H. Gamble, James A. Laidlaw, D. McCrimmon, J. M. Scott and N. Gordon.

Ushers—Allan Cameron, W. T. Carruthers, J. T. Tennant, L. Trickey.

Auditors—W. A. Gilmour, R. A. McLelland.

The Board of Managers was authorized to pay accounts for the Sabbath School, from the church funds, to the amount of $100.

A committee, composed of Rev. Robert Laird, Sheriff Dana, John M. Gill, Thomas Wilkinson and Robert Laidlaw, was appointed to examine the title deed under which the church property is held and procure the necessary information with a view to ascertaining what steps should be taken to bring the management of the affairs of the congregation into harmony with the uniform practice of the Presbyterian Church in Canada, said committee to report to a congregational meeting to be held for the purpose of receiving and considering such report.

A vote of thanks was tendered the Board of Trustees for their excellent and careful management of the temporal affairs of the church during the year.

The meeting was then closed with the benediction by the pastor, after which refreshments were served and a pleasant time spent in social intercourse.

A special meeting of the congregation was held on the evening of Dec. 1900, to receive a report of the committee appointed to inquire into the title deeds of the church property with a view to making such changes therein as will bring the management of the affairs of the congregation into harmony with the uniform practice of the Presbyterian Church in Canada.

After a short session of prayer and praise the meeting was organized with the pastor in the chair and R. Laidlaw, Secretary.

Rev Mr. Laird explained very fully the action that had been taken by the committee in regard to the special matter placed in their charge.

Moved by Thomas Wilkinson, seconded by John M. Gill;

Whereas, The First Presbyterian Church of the Town of Brockville is a congregation in connection and communion with the Presbyterian Church in Canada;

And Whereas, By the act respecting the union of certain Presbyterian Churches therein named, passed in the 38th year of Her Majesty's reign, it is provided by section 3 that congregations may from time to time alter or vary any of the provisions contained in the trust deeds under which their property is held, or in their constitutions which relate to the mode in which their affairs and property shall be managed or regulated and to the persons who shall be entitled to take part in such management or to vote at meetings of the congregation on questions affecting the affairs and property of the congregation or the management thereof;

And Whereas, The congregation hold the land upon which their church is erected under a certain indenture, dated on the 19th day of November, 1847, from the Rev. Wm. Smart to John McLean and others, and which contains certain provisions or trusts;

And Whereas, They also hold certain other property adjoining under a certain indenture, dated on the 12th day of April, 1871, from the Rev. Wm. Smart to David Wylie and others, and which also contains certain provisions and trusts;

And Whereas, It is desirable to alter and vary the said trust deeds and the constitution of said congregation so as to bring the same into harmony with the present law and practice of the Presbyterian Church in Canada;

And Whereas, Due notice has been given of the holding of this meeting and of the business to be transacted thereat;

Be It Therefore Resolved,

1. That the constitution and rules of procedure of the said congregation of the First Presbyterian Church in the Town of Brockville shall be those laid down in the rules and forms of procedure in the Church Courts of the Presbyterian Church in Canada, adopted by the General Assembly in 1889.

2. That the management of the temporal affairs of the congregation, including the care of the church and manse property, shall be intrusted to a board of nine managers, three retiring annually, in accordance with the said rules and forms of procedure.

3· That the rules respecting the call and settlement and resignation of the pastor and all matters relating to the pastoral office and eldership contained in said rules and forms of procedure are hereby adopted.

4. All the business of the congregation shall be conducted in accordance with the said rules.

5. The clauses contained in the said indenture of the 19th of November, 1847 numbered secondly, third, fourth, fifth, sixth and seventh, and the clauses numbered second, third, fourth, fifth and sixth contained in the said indenture of 12th April, 1871, and any and all clauses, trusts or provisoes inconsistent herewith, are hereby repealed and cancelled, and the following taken from the model form of deed on pages 129, 130 and 131 of the said rules and forms of procedure are hereby substituted as being the trusts upon which the Trustees hold the parcels of land mentioned in the said indenture of 19th of November, 1847, and 12th of April, 1871.

"And it is hereby declared that the said parties of the second part (the trustees), and their successors, shall hold the said lands for the sole nse and benefit of the said congregation, for the site of a church or meeting house. burial ground and residence for the minister (as the said congregation may from time to time direct), and for the support and maintenance of public worship and the propagation of Christian knowledge, according to the doctrines, discipline and modes of worship of the said Presbyterian Church in Canada, and subject to the provisions of the said acts. And upon further trust that the said parties of the second part, and their successors, shall and will, well and truly, obey, perform and fulfill, and permit and suffer to be obeyed, performed and fulfilled, with respect to the said lands; and to any church or other building or buildings now erected, or to be erected upon the said lands; or to any burial ground, if the said lands or any part thereof shall be used as a burial ground, the lawful orders and directions respectively of the said congregation, the

Deacons' Court, if any, the Kirk Session of the said congregation, the Presbytery and Synod respectively, within whose bounds and under whose inspection and ecclesiastical jurisdiction the said congregation shall from time to time be, and the General Assembly or other Supreme Court of the Presbyterian Church in Canada. And with respect to the election and appointment of new trustees, it is declared that a general meeting of the said congregation shall be held on the fourth Wednesday in January in the year one thousand nine hundred and one, and on the fourth Wednesday in January in every fifth year thereafter, called by a written notice, read to the congregation at the close of public worship on each of the two next preceding Sabbaths by the officiating minister or other person appointed to read the same; but if, from any cause, the meeting shall not be held on that day, then it shall be called in like manner for some other day at the request of the Trustees or of seven members of the congregation in full communion; and any such meeting may be adjourned as occasion shall require; and at such regular or adjourned meeting the said congregation shall elect and appoint five Trustees by the votes of the majority of the members of the congregation in full communion then present; such Trustees to be members of the Presbyterian Church in Canada in full communion. And it is hereby further declared that the said Trustees shall respectively hold office until the appointment of their successors, except in case of death, resignation or ceasing to be a member of the Presbyterian Church in Canada in full communion; and that in case any Trustee shall, during his term of office, die, resign or cease to be a member of the Presbyterian Church in Canada in full communion, the remaining Trustees shall have all the powers of the full board; and shall, for all purposes of these presents, be the Trustees of the said congregation, unless the congregation shall think fit to appoint a new Trustee or new Trustees in the place of any Trustee or Trustees so dying, resigning or ceasing to be a member of the Presbyterian Church in Canada in full communion; but the said congregation may, at any special meeting called by written notice, read to the congregation by the officiating minister or other person appointed to read the same, at the close of public worship, on each of the two next preceding Sabbaths, which notice shall be given at the request of the remaining Trustees or of any seven members of the congregation in full communion, appoint by votes of a majority of the members of the congregation in full communion then present, a new Trustee or new Trustees, to fill for the residue of such term of office any vacancy or vacancies caused as aforesaid. And it is hereby further declared that a minute of every such election or appointment, whether made at a regular meeting, or at any adjourned or special meeting, shall be entered in a book to be kept for the purpose, and shall be signed by the person who presides at the meeting; and such minute so signed shall, for all purposes connected with these presents, be sufficient evidence of the fact that the persons therein named were elected and appointed at such meeting; but the omission or neglect to make or sign such minute, shall not invalidate the election or appointment. And it is hereby further declared that in case at any time the said Trusteeship shall for any reason become wholly vacant, so that there shall be no remaining Trustee the Moderator and Clerk of the Presbytery, within whose bounds and under whose jurisdiction the said congregation shall be, shall thereupon forthwith become and be Trustees under these presents until others are duly appointed, and at any time thereafter the Presbytery may cause notice to be given from the pulpit at each diet of worship on two consecutive Sabbaths, requiring the said congregation to proceed to the appointment of new Trustees; and if the said congregation shall not in the meantime have appointed new Trustees in the manner hereinbefore provided, it shall be lawful for the said Presbytery, after four weeks from the last giving of such notice, to appoint new Trustees to act for the residue of the then current term of office; every such appointment to be made by resolution duly entered in the minutes of the Presbytery, and communicated to the congregation by notice from the pulpit; and the Trustees so appointed shall from the time of communication of their appointment to the congregation be the Trustees for the residue of such term of office for the purpose of these presents. Provided also, and it is hereby declared, that if at any time there shall cease to be an organized congregation entitled to the use, benefit and enjoyment of the said lands, then and as often as that shall occur, it shall be lawful for the Presbytery within the bounds of which the said land is situated, to fill any vacancy in the said Board of Trustees, and the said lands shall thenceforth be held subject to such trusts and for such purposes for the benefit of the Presbyterian Church in Canada, as the General Assembly or other Supreme Court of the church may declare, limit or appoint." Carried.

Moved by R. Laidlaw, seconded by R. H. Gamble, That the Secretary of this congregational meeting be instructed to hand the resolutions passed at this meeting affecting the property and affairs of First Church to the Session of the Church, with a request that they be transmitted to the Presbytery of Brockville praying for the sanction of the said Presbytery to the changes, embodied in said resolutions, in the Trusts and Rules and Forms of Procedure under which the congregation of First Church hold their property and manage their affairs. Carried.

Moved by R. H. Gamble, seconded by Allan Cameron, That the resolution changing the Title Deed of the Church be registered in the Registry Office for the County of Leeds. Carried.

Moved by Allan Cameron, seconded by Wm. Sutherland, That the management of the temporal affairs of the Church be continued in the present Board of Trustees until their successors are elected under the provisions of the new deed. Carried.

The meeting closed with the benediction by the Pastor.

In accordance with the above, the resolutions passed at the meeting of the congregation on Dec. 5th, 1900, making certain alterations in the trust deeds under which the church property was held, were presented to Brockville Presbytery at a meeting held at Prescott on Dec. 11th, 1900, and were then and there sanctioned by that church court.

SESSION REPORT, 1900.

The year 1900 has been one of earnest and substantial work in our congregational life. God has been with his people and we remember with gratitude the way in which He has led us and the strength he has given the workers in His kingdom. Discouragements have not been wanting, but we have much cause to thank God and take courage.

At the beginning of the year the members in full communion numbered 380 By profession of faith 12 have been added during the year, 15 by certificates from other churches, and 15 names were re-entered on the Roll. 7 have been removed by certificate, 3 by death and 9 by revision of the Roll. The present membership is 403. The ordinance of Baptism was administered to 4 adults and 11 children.

The attendance at the Worship of the Sanctuary has on the whole been encouraging, but the mind of the Session is that the parents should take earnest and immediate steps towards securing a larger attendance of children at the church service on Sabbath morning. Undoubtedly, too, we need greater loyalty in remembering our Lord at His Table and a deeper and more definite interest in the mid-week prayer meeting. If our people entered more heartily into the means of grace their lives would grow richer and more Christ-like.

We are pleased to note a spirit of earnestness and progress in our Sabbath School work. The attendance of the scholars has been larger and more regular, the teachers have shewn their accustomed fidelity, and the study of the Shorter Catechism has to a growing extent occupied the attention of the school. In the coming year memorizing of Scripture will be urged upon the children, and the Session would impress upon the parents the importance of their aiding in every possible way in the advancement of Bible study and in the cultivation of religious life in the home.

The year has been one of heavy financial obligation. It was feared that the large payments on the church debt and the generous contributions of many of our people to the Century Fund would interfere seriously with contributions to schemes of the church The good response shows that our people have remained loyal to our advancing missionary work. The appropriations are as follows :

    Home Mission Fund $110.00
    Augmentation of Stipend Fund................ 110.00

> Foreign Mission Fund 110.00
> French Evangelization Fund 30.00
> Montreal College Fund 15.00
> Queen's   "   " 30.00
> Manitoba   "   " 15.00
> Widows' and Orphans' Fund 25.00
> Aged and Infirm Ministers' Fund 25.00
> Assembly Fund 9.70
> Special India Famine Fund 10.00
> Special Augmentation contribution 40.00

These contributions from the congregation alone amount to $529.70. When to this are added the Missionary Offerings of the Sabbath School, W. F. M. S., Mission Band and Endeavor Societies, the total contributions from all sources for the Schemes are $1056.70 in comparison with $1020 the preceding year.

The Session desire to put on record their gratification at the changes recently made by the congregation in the Trust Deeds of the church by which its constitution and regulations have been brought into harmony with the practice of the Presbyterian Church in Canada.

We would assure those of our members who have been bereaved or afflicted in any way during the year of our deep sympathy and commend them to the grace and comfort of God.

Our heartiest thanks are given to those who have served Christ and his Church in our various organizations and in the service of praise, and we confidently hope that the labors and the blessings of this passing year will give us all stronger faith and growing energy for the work of the New Year and the New Century.

JOHN M. GILL,   ROBT. LAIRD,
    Session Clerk.   Moderator of Session.

IN MEMORIAM.

1900.

Mrs. George Campbell.
Mrs. William Shearer.
Mrs. Joseph Robb
Mr. Thomas Beattie.
Miss Janet Wilkinson.
Mr. George Warwick.
Mr. Andrew Cook.
Mrs. McCracken.
Infant child of Jas. Taggart.
Infant child of Jas. H. Stewart.

BOARD OF TRUSTEES' REPORT.

The Board of Trustees of the First Presbyterian Church in presenting their report for the year 1900 beg to congratulate both pastor and people upon the good work that has been accomplished. The contributions from all sources for all purposes for the year amount to over $12,000, which includes $7,000 paid on the subscriptions to the debt fund. The subscribers to this latter fund have responded to the calls made upon them with commendable promptness, and there is no doubt that a year hence the mortgage debt upon the church property will be entirely removed. Being rid of the debt and the consequent heavy annual interest liability which it incurred will place the congregation in an excellent position financially and also, we hope, clear the way for greater efforts in other departments of church work. Taking into consideration the heavy tax placed upon the members by their payments to the debt fund and the many other unusual demands made upon their liberality during the year, the contributions to ordinary revenue have been very satisfactory.

Your Board view with much favor the changes that have been made in the trust deeds, which place the control of the church property and the management of the temporal affairs of the congregation upon a different basis from what has hitherto obtained, and believe that these will be advantageous in furthering the best interests of the congregation.

We have much pleasure in presenting with the annual report this year a brief historical sketch of the church covering the period of 89 years that has elapsed since the date of its organization in 1811, down to the present, giving excellent portraits of all those who have ministered to the people during that time, also views of the different churches that have occupied the site where the present handsome edifice stands.

The congregation of First Church has an honored and historic past, full of records of great things done in the service of the Master. Let us all resolve at the opening of a new century to increase our efforts and seek in every way possible to prove ourselves worthy of the splendid heritage that has been handed down to us.

R. LAIDLAW,
Secretary.

THOS. WILKINSON,
Chairman.

FINANCIAL SECRETARY'S STATEMENT.

DR.

Plate Collections ....$	422.99
From Envelopes for ordinary expenditure, 1900, including part of arrears due 1899, as per detailed list...............................	3038.89
Collection for Hospital	44.34
	$3506.22

CR.

Amount paid Thos. Wilkinson, Church Treasurer,
from envelopes and plate collection.........   3506.22

JAMES T. TENNANT,
Financial Secretary.

Special collection for Brockville General Hospital, taken at Union Sacramental service, $117.21.

DETAILED LIST OF CONTRIBUTORS.

	Weekly Offerings	Church Schemes	Debt Fund.
Armour, Robert	$ 6 60		
Armstrong, W. H.........	18 20		
Abbott, Albert.........	20 00	$ 2 00	$ 30 00
Burrows, G. H.........	32 00		
Brownlee, J. H	20 00		
Buckman, E. A.	26 00	10 00	30 00
Bates, J. W......	1 75		
Buell, C. H	31 20	5 00	20 00
Bailey, Nancy.	2 10	25	
Bowyer, Daniel.....	6 90		
Bellamy, Mrs. H. H.........	10 80	2 00	
Brown, George H.........	13 00		10 00
Brown, Mrs George H.		2 00	
Bisset, E. H.........			10 00
Buckman, George			10 00
Buckman, Mrs. E. A.........			10 00
Clark, H. A.....	15 00		20 00
Cossitt, Newton, Sr.	100 00	25 00	800 00
Cumbers, T. W.....	15 60	1 00	10 00
Cossitt, G. M	100 00	5 00	
Carruthers, W. T	12 25		
Cowan, Mrs. Norman.........	4 40		
Cameron, Miss Jennie.........	6 00		10 00
Carruthers, William.....	20 80	10 00	
Cameron, Allan.....	31 20	25 00	80 00

FINANCIAL SECRETARY'S STATEMENT.

	Weekly Offerings	Church Schemes.	Debt Fund.
Cameron, Mrs. Allan		$ 10 00	
Clark, Miss R	$ 6 00	1 00	
Colborne, Ida	4 00		
Cormack, John	13 50		
Comstock, W. H	156 00		1740 00
Clayes, Mrs. E. D	26 00		
Cole, Mrs. James	5 40		
Cossitt, F. B	26 00	5 00	30 00
Cossitt, C. S	31 20	5 00	200 00
Coons, Miss	4 90	1 00	
Curry, William	7 80		
Carruthers, Mrs	1 90		
Culbert, Mrs. John	12 50		
Campbell, James	7 75		10 00
Campbell, Miss	18 20	1 00	15 00
Carruthers, Mrs. W. T		1 00	
Cole, Mrs. Henry		2 00	5 00
Cossitt, Cora N			10 00
Cossitt, Francis A			10 00
Culbert, John			15 00
Cole, Delilah			5 00
Dowsley, J. M	20 00		15 00
Dunn, Thomas	10 40		10 00
Dickey, J. J	15 50		50 00
Dowsley, M.	13 00		
Dudley, George	28 00		30 00
Dana, George A	52 00		60 00
Dowsley, Mrs. John	4 75		
Dick, Hugh	7 50		
Dewey, Mrs. C I	5 30		10 00
Davidson, W. J			15 00
Dewey, G. K	7 95		
Denaut, Mrs	13 25		20 00
Dodds, Mrs. Margaret Dodds	9 50	2 00	5 00
Dudley, Mrs. George		50	
Eggleston, W. A	6 50		
Easton, J	3 45		
Edwards Mrs	90		
Ellis. J. F	5 00	1 00	
Flemming, Miss M	2 75		
Ferguson. Peter	10 00		10 00
Fulford, Mrs. James	6 00		30 00
Foster, Olive	10	1 00	
French, C. H	15 60	5 20	10 00
Fulford, Mrs. John	13 00		20 00
Foxton, Alex	13 00		
Fullerton, Adam	32 50		40 00
Fulford, F. H			10 00
Gill, John M	104 00		500 00
Gill, Mr. and Mrs. J. M.		80 00	
Gill, Bessie C		5 00	30 00
Gill, M. Berta		5 00	30 00
Gill, Annie P		5 00	30 00
Gill, Robt. James		5 00	30 00
Gilmour, Albert	26 00		50 00
Gordon, N	10 50	2 00	
Gilmour, W. A	39 00		150 00
Gilmour, Mrs. W. A		4 00	
Graham, Miss	7 50		20 00

FINANCIAL SECRETARY'S STATEMENT. 37

	Weekly Offerings	Church Schemes	Debt Fund.
Going, H. W.	12 00		20 00
Gordon, Mrs. Robert	8 05	1 00	
Grant, Robert	8 15	1 00	
Gilmour, James H.	39 00		270 00
Goodison, Robert	10 00		
Garrett, A. W.	13 00		5 00
Gollan, Mrs. L. J.	3 90		
Gamble, R. H.	20 90		30 00
Gamble, F. W.	5 30	2 00	20 00
Gamble, Mr. and Mrs. R. H.		5 00	
Goldthorpe, Mrs.	95		
Gordon, Miss A.		3 00	
Grant, Jennie		50	
Gardner, J. Gill			10 00
Hayes, D. F.	19 20	2 00	20 00
Hutcheson, A. R.	2 60		
Hillis Hance	13 00	2 00	
Heyward, J.	4 55	1 00	
Hamilton, David	13 50	1 00	5 00
Harding, Mrs. T J. B.	3 00		10 00
Haig, Alice	9 75	3 00	
Harding, Ernest, M.D.	15 00		
Hare, Thomas	2 00	3 00	
Higgins, J. P.	2 55		
Haig, Jane	8 20	2 00	
Hillis, C.	3 65		5 00
Hay, Charles J	17 10		15 00
Hillis, Herman		1 00	
Ingles, William	6 00		
Johnston, Robert	1 62	1 00	1 00
Johnston, L.	13 00	1 00	30 00
Kyle, Mrs. John	10 40		
Kelley, Arthur	2 55		
King, William	26 00		
Kilgour, Peter	8 25		
Kilborne, Mrs.	6 00		
Kelley, W. L.	13 00		5 00
Kilborn, W. E.			10 00
Kyle, W. H.			10 00
Kilborn, Luther			5 00
Kilborn, Lydia			5 00
Lafayette, G. G.	13 00		15 00
Lewis, James	5 40		
Lanskail, James S.	20 80	2 00	10 00
Laidlaw, James A	13 00		10 00
Laird, Mrs. R.	7 75		
Lalonde, Mrs.	20 00		
Links, Misses	5 20		50
Laidlaw, Robert	13 00	2 00	20 00
Leckie, William	6 70		
Loucks, Mrs. W. E	1 30		
Laird, Rev. R. and Mrs		50 00	
Lewis, Mrs. J.		1 00	30 00
Laird, Rev. Robert			90 00
Laughlin, J. H.			10 00
Moore, James	26 00		
Menish, John	18 20	3 00	15 00
Murray, G. B.	16 00		
Mead, Robert	14 20		20 00

FINANCIAL SECRETARY'S STATEMENT.

	Weekly Offerings	Church Schemes.	Debt Fund.
Morey, R. D.	5 20		
Marquis, T. G.	7 75		
Meachim, Mrs. J.	2 75		
Mott, Mrs.	1 75		
Montgomery, W.	26 00		
Milroy, James	1 30		
Miller, Fred J.	1 75		
Maxwell, Mrs. James	1 65		
MacLaren, David	7 00	2 00	
MacLaren, Mrs. David		2 00	
MacLaren, John	104 00	100 00	900 00
Macdonald, John	13 00	1 00	5 00
Mackenzie, Allan	18 00		
Mackenzie, Mrs. J. A.		1 00	
Mackenzie, Susie M.		2 00	
Menish, J. Stanley			15 00
Mackenzie, John A.			45 00
McCullough, George	11 00		
McKay, William	9 45	1 00	
McCrady, F. G.	13 00		
McCrady, A. G.	6 00		
McGraw, John	13 00	50	
McCaw, Mrs. Wm.	5 40		
McElhinney, Mrs. J.	8 00		15 00
McLelland, R. A.	35 00		50 00
McCrimmon, D.	13 55	2 00	5 00
McCullough, D.	9 75		
McArthur, Wm.	20 80	1 00	20 00
McCormack, Mrs. M. A.	5 20	2 00	5 00
McMillan, P. K.	1 40		
McPherson, A. J.	11 25		
McCoo, Archie	3 20		
McMillan, M.	8 00		
McEwan, Mrs. T.	15 00	2 00	
McCrady, C. H.	13 00		
McNaughten, Dr.	5 00		
McDermott, Mrs. M.	1 55		
McNish, Alonzo	2 50		
Nicolson, George	5 70		
Nicolson, W. K.	5 77		
Old, Mrs. M. J.	6 50	1 00	
Olds, Miss	3 00		
Purvis, Robert	15 45		10 00
Page, E. L.	16 25		
Page, A. G.	13 00		
Powell, James D.	40 00		
Publow, Mrs. John	12 50		5 00
Page, J. A.	13 00		
Perry, James	4 75		5 00
Patterson, Thomas	31 20	10 00	30 00
Robertson, T. F., M. D.	13 50		20 00
Reynolds, Mrs. S.	13 00		
Reid, Robert	16 05		10 00
Robinson, Mrs.	5 00		
Russell, J.	8 10		
Rowe, C. A.	4 00		
Rappell, George	1 30		
Rose, Lewis	2 00		
Robertson, Fred	4 70		

FINANCIAL SECRETARY'S STATEMENT.

	Weekly Offerings	Church Schemes	Debt Fund.
Robertson, James	15 00	1 00	
Rogers, W. N.	6 25		
Robb, Joseph	8 00		
Rowe, W.	1 25		
Reid, Mrs. R.		1 00	
Reynolds, James			20 00
Sutherland, W.	26 00	2 00	30 00
Storey, T. J.	26 00		30 00
Stewart, Mrs. J. H.	5 10		
Seaman, Mrs. B. R.	7 80		
Shearer, W.	26 00	5 00	60 00
Stagg, Mrs. A. F.	15 60		30 00
Stewart, H. A	13 00		10 00
Soper, Henry	13 00		30 00
Scott, Mrs. J.	13 00		
Stewart, Jane	5 10		
Smith, Mrs. G.	15 60	1 00	15 00
Stewart, Alex	19 20		
Scott, James H.	13 00		20 00
Stewart, Mildred	2 00		
St. John, Estella	5 20		3 00
Swarts, A. H.	15 00		10 00
Seaman, H. S.	20 00	5 00	45 00
Starr, Miss	13 00	1 00	3 34
Steele, Mrs. J. C.	13 25		
Saunders, Mary	2 00	1 00	
Semple, Lizzie	1 20		
Steele, J. C.			10 00
Smart, A L			20 00
Scott, J. M			10 00
Tennant, J. T.	52 00	10 00	180 00
Taplin, H	20 80		60 00
Tennant, G. A.	5 35		
Tomlison, Mrs	1 15		
Tompkins, Mrs. C. A.	6 00		5 00
Turkington, M.	8 60		
Taylor, James	4 10		
Trickey, L. C	5 25		
Trickey, E. L	5 25		
Trusdale, O.	2 40		
Timlick, F.	10		
Tompkins, Stuart R.		1 00	
Tennant, Mrs. G. A.		50	
Trickey, Mrs.		1 00	
Urquhart, James	85		
Van Dusen, J.	9 15	1 00	
Wilkinson, Thos.	40 00	5 00	180 00
Worden, Mrs.	26 00		10 00
Wright, S. H.	13 00	1 0	5 00
Walsh, Mrs. J. M.	25 00	2 00	68 50
Wright, A. S	13 00		
Wilson, Mrs. S.	5 60		
Wilkinson, C.	8 75		15 00
Wilkinson, A A	10 00		
Weatherspun, J.	10		
Watson, Mrs. S. J.	5 45		5 00
Wright, W. J.	31 70		
Wilkinson, C. T.			10 00
Y. P. C. E. Society, Juniors			30 00

	Weekly Offerings	Church Schemes.	Debt Fund.
Y. P. C. E. Society, Seniors			24 50
A Friend		5 00	
A Friend		2 00	
Unknown source		25	
Young, William E	1 60		
Young, M. S	50		
Friends (for augmentation)		40 00	
Total	$3 38 89	$ 529 70	$7030 84

DEBT FUND REPORT.

BROCKVILLE, Jan. 1, 1901.

Amount paid on subscriptions to church debt fund......... $7030 84
Paid Thos. Wilkinson, Church Treasurer................. 7000 00

Balance cash on hand................................. $ 30 84

JAMES H. GILMOUR, Treasurer.

TREASURER'S REPORT.

1900.	Dr.		
To balance on hand		$ 137	89
Received from J. T. Tennant, Financial Secretary		3506	22
Schemes of church		529	70
J. H. Gilmour (Debt Fund)		7000	00
Note discounted		500	00
A. G. Dobbie & Co		2	70
Old blinds (sold)		3	00
Unknown sources		60	00
		$11739	60
To balance on hand Jan. 1, 1901		$ 136	83

1900.	Cr.		
By Rev. R. Laird		$ 1600	00
Pulpit supply		93	55
Choir		577	00
Wm. McArthur		200	00
H. A. Stewart (executor), rent		300	00
R. A. McLelland (Sunday School)		105	02
Interest		465	00
Insurance, church and manse		87	25
Presbytery dues		26	25
Paid on church mortgage		7000	00
Brockville General Hospital		40	00
Brockville Light and Power Co		114	54
Brockville Water Department		33	82
C. W. Johnston, gas inspector		3	00
Mrs. Doran		1	00
Canada Central Coal Co		128	35
Town taxes		54	75
Recorder Printing Co		30	75
Wm. Gray		6	53
A. G. Dobbie & Co		18	31
F. H. Fulford		14	40

By G. Ross	2	50
J. L. Orme & Son	1	50
J. W. Ridgeway	1	45
J. T. Tennant	50	00
G. D. McDougall	4	00
Mrs. Roswell		50
Relief fund (A. Cameron)	15	00
The Rathbun Co	1	15
Allan Cameron	5	40
A. Fullerton	3	06
T. Dowell	12	19
W. H. Harrison	16	80
Central Canada Coal Co	60	00
Schemes of church	529	70
Balance	136	83
	$11739	60

LIABILITIES.

Mortgage on church $	3000	00
Mortgage on manse	1300	00
Two notes discounted	1200	00
Central Canada Coal Co	71	60
	$ 5571	60

I hereby certify that I have examined the Cash Book and report of the Treasurer for the year 1900 and find the vouchers for amounts paid out, and also the additions and balance correct.

W. A. GILMOUR,

Jan. 16, 1901.   Auditor.

SABBATH SCHOOL REPORT.
For the Year Ending Dec. 31st, 1900.

OFFICERS.

WM SUTHERLAND,	Superintendent.
CHAS. J. HAY,	Asst. Superintendent.
R. A. MCLELLAND,	Treasurer.
WM. K. NICOLSON,	Librarian.
L. SUTHERLAND,	Asst. Librarian.
G. A. TENNANT,	Secretary.
FREDERICK GAMBLE,	Asst. Secretary.

TEACHERS.

†Miss Robertson, †Mrs. Allan Cameron, *Miss M McEwan, Mrs. G. A. Tennant, †Miss Cormack, Miss B Moray, Mrs. J. Menish, Miss L. Stagg, Miss P. Dewey, Miss M. Coons, Miss J. McDonald, Miss M. Loucks, Miss J. McArthur, †Miss Denaut, Miss M. Moore, Miss L. Purvis, Miss Carrie Fulford, Mrs. J. Moore, Mr. John M. Gill, Mr. N. Gordon, Mr. C. J. Hay, Mr. A. Cameron, †Mr. J. M. Scott, Mr. R. Moray.

†Resigned. *Left Town.

TEACHERS OF CHINESE MISSION.

Miss H. Davies, Miss M. Abbott, Mrs. Mott, Miss K. C. Davis, Miss B. Purves, Mrs. Gollan, Miss Ruth Tomlinson, Miss Horton, Miss Tompkins and Miss A. McCullough.

NEW TEACHERS INSTALLED DURING THE YEAR.

Miss Stewart, Miss Johnston, Miss B. Gill, Mrs. Brownlee, Mr. R A. McLelland and Rev. Mr. Laird.

MEMBERSHIP.

Scholars on roll Jan. 1, 1900	214
New scholars during the year	104
Chinese Mission (membership)	6
	324
Scholars left during year	41
Scholars on roll, including Bible Class and Chinese Mission, Dec. 31st, 1900	283

ATTENDANCE.

Total attendance of scholars	8407
" " teachers	1187
" " officers	295
" " visitors	225
	10114

Average attendance per Sabbath of 165 scholars, 23 teachers, 6 officers and 4 visitors. Total 198

Total collections for the year amounted to $187 66

An average per Sabbath of 3 68

The collections were devoted to sustaining Mr. V. M. Purdy, Home Missionary at Salmon Arm, B. C.

The sum of $51.08 was realized for the Century Fund from the banks furnished the children by one of the members of our school.

It is very gratifying to know that a large number of the scholars will repeat the shorter catechism.

There has been a marked increase in all departments of our school.

The following are the names of the scholars who attended Sabbath School every Sabbath during the year: Allie Sutherland, Jakie Miller, Ernie Major, Victor Milroy, John Russell, Annie Russell, Mamie Gordcn, Gertie Carruthers, Beatrice Carruthers, Charles Russell, Willie Carruthers, Cassie Cook, Allie Miller, Robie Major, Leonard Vanduzen, Davie Purves, Jessie Purves, Maggie Milroy, Kathleen Cameron, Ogilvie Russell, Pansy Baverstock, Lizzie Cormack, Jos. Russell, Grace Kilgour, Jean Kilgour and Tena Kilgour.

The following are the names of those attending every Sabbath but one: Lou Goldthorpe, Clara Steele and Hattie Steele.

We are pleased to note that ten of our scholars united with the church this year.

The officers and teachers feel deeply indebted to Mr. Newton Gossitt, Sr., who has so liberally from year to year furnished means to purchase prizes for the scholars who attended every Sabbath during the year, and also to Mr. F. H. Fulford and the members of his orchestra who have furnished us with excellent music, which has helped greatly in making our school attractive and delightful.

Our annual flower service, anniversary and picnic were held as usual to the delight of those attending.

G. A. TENNANT,
Secretary.

TREASURER'S STATEMENT.

In Account With First Church Sabbath School.

1900.	Dr.		
Subscriptions to orchestra		$ 5	50
Excursion		47	25
Picnic		44	60
N. Cossitt, for prizes		10	00
T. Wilkinson, Treasurer		105	02
Century fund coll		51	08
Mrs. Moore's class		7	12
Mr. Morey's class		24	36
Y. P. S. C. E.		15	00
Y. P. S. C. E. Juniors		10	00
Colls. from school		163	24
Special coll. re mission fund		27	20
Interest		1	84
Balance			03
		$512	24

1900.	Cr.		
New Year's Rally expenses, 1-5 exp		$	80
Convention expenses		2	25
B. D. Steacy, wire netting, July, '98		1	50
F. H. Fulford, hymnals		27	45
N Cossitt		4	80
A. Cameron, — Anniversary		8	10
C. H. Buell, — and Picnic		5	26
Abbott, Grant & Co. — supplies.		2	11
Picnic and Sunday School expenses		2	50
Recorder, $5.35, $3		8	35
Smart Manufacturing Co, music stands		4	50
" " hooks		1	20
Greene & Co, prizes		3	00
Revell & Co., records		1	03
Presbyterian Pub. Co		36	25
Excursion boat		25	00
Cole Manufacturing Co., prizes		9	96
F. H. Fulford, for services		10	00
Boat for picnic		50	00
Century fund coll		51	08
R. H. Warden, D. D. for Missionary		250	00
Picnic expenses		7	10
		$512	24

REPORT OF THE WOMAN'S FOREIGN MISSIONARY SOCIETY FOR 1900.

OFFICERS.

Mrs. R. Laidlaw,	President.
Mrs. Gill,	
" W. A. Gilmour,	Vice-Presidents.
" A. Cameron,	
Mrs. Laird,	Corresponding Secretary.
Mrs. Menish,	Recording Secretary.
Mrs. Patterson,	Treasurer.
Mrs. Taplin,	Sec'y Missionary Tidings.
Miss Dewey,	Organist.

The regular monthly meeting is held on the first Thursday of each month at 3 p. m., in the ladies' parlor. No. of members, 47. No. of leaflets distributed, 60. Through the efforts of our Society $138 was contributed and sent to Dr. Warden for the India Famine Fund, and $205 for Missions. Sewing meetings were held and clothing and new material valued at $42.35 were also sent to the Mission at Pipestone Reserve.

Mrs. Menish,
Rec. Sec'y.

REPORT OF YOUNG LADIES' MISSION BAND, 1900.

OFFICERS FOR 1901.

Mrs. Scott,	President.
Mrs. Gamble,	1st Vice-President.
Miss Dewey,	2nd Vice-President.
Miss McDonald,	Treasurer.
Miss Graham,	Secretary.

The regular monthly meeting is held on the second Thursday of each month, in the ladies' parlor. No. of members, 25. Average attendance 16. Contributions to Missions, $72.

H. Graham,
Secretary.

REPORT OF Y. P. S. C. E.

The work we have done during the year 1900 has, we feel, not been in vain. Our meetings, which have been held regularly every Monday evening, have been of a very helpful character and, as a rule, very well attended. We have held two social evenings, also "A Missionary Tour Around the World," when Rev. Mr. Laird, Rev. Mr. Clendinnen and G. P. Graham, M.P.P, took us across the continent to Vancouver, and Rev. Mr. Crummy took us through Japan. These tours were very interesting.

We have twenty-one Active and three Associate members. Four of our number moved away from town. We have had the pleasure of taking into our Society three new members. The total attendance for the year was 1789 ; average 36.

The Flower Committee during the year distributed to the sick and infirm 250 bouquets and plants, with a message of peace and comfort attached and an earnest prayer that some lives may be brightened. Our Calling Committee has made 106 calls during the year.

Our Society raised by voluntary contribution $40 for running expenses. Besides this, they have raised for Missionary purposes $5 ; $10 were given to Queen's College Missionary Society, and $4 10 to the India Famine Fund.

At Christmas baskets, well filled with good things, were distributed among those who may not have been as bountifully provided for as ourselves.

As the new century comes upon us, we start the work with renewed energy to keep our motto, "For Christ and the Church," ever before us.

W. K. NICOLSON,
President.

MISS EFFIE PAUL,
Rec. Secretary.

REPORT OF J. S. C. E.

The closing year of the century is past, and we are delighted to be able to say that in no year of our history has the work of our Society been so successful.

Our membership at the opening of the year was 98; at the close 103. The total attendance 2613; average 51.

The work has been pushed with energy by the members, and it is pleasing to know that many an effort has been crowned with success.

The voluntary contributions at our Sunday morning meetings amounted to $14, which is used for carrying on our work The Missionary givings have trebled those of any previous year of our history. We received from Missionary Barrels, $15; from sale of stamps $7; and individual offerings to the extent of $8; making a total for Missionary purposes this year of $30.

The Sunshine Committee have distributed over 200 bouquets of flowers to the sick. Papers were sent to a needy Sabbath School, and books have been made and distributed.

Our Social Committee have been active, and by their efforts we were enabled to give one share amounting to $30 to the debt fund of our church. In many other ways have we assisted.

We desire also to place in this report a financial statement, which is as follows:

Received from all Sources, Collections, concerts, missions, etc....$91 00
Paid out to debt fund................................ 30 00
    Missionary in British Columbia................ 10 00
    Queen's Missionary Association............... 5 00
    Library for Sailors on St. Lawrence........... 5 00
    Missionary work............................. 10 00
    For carrying on our work and opening up new work 24 00
    Balance on hand............................ 7 00
                                                                     ——$91 00

Trusting that the same encouragement and support will be given us in the future we press forward in His name.

                        ROBT. D. MORAY, Superintendent,
                        MISS B. I. MORAY, Asst. Supt.

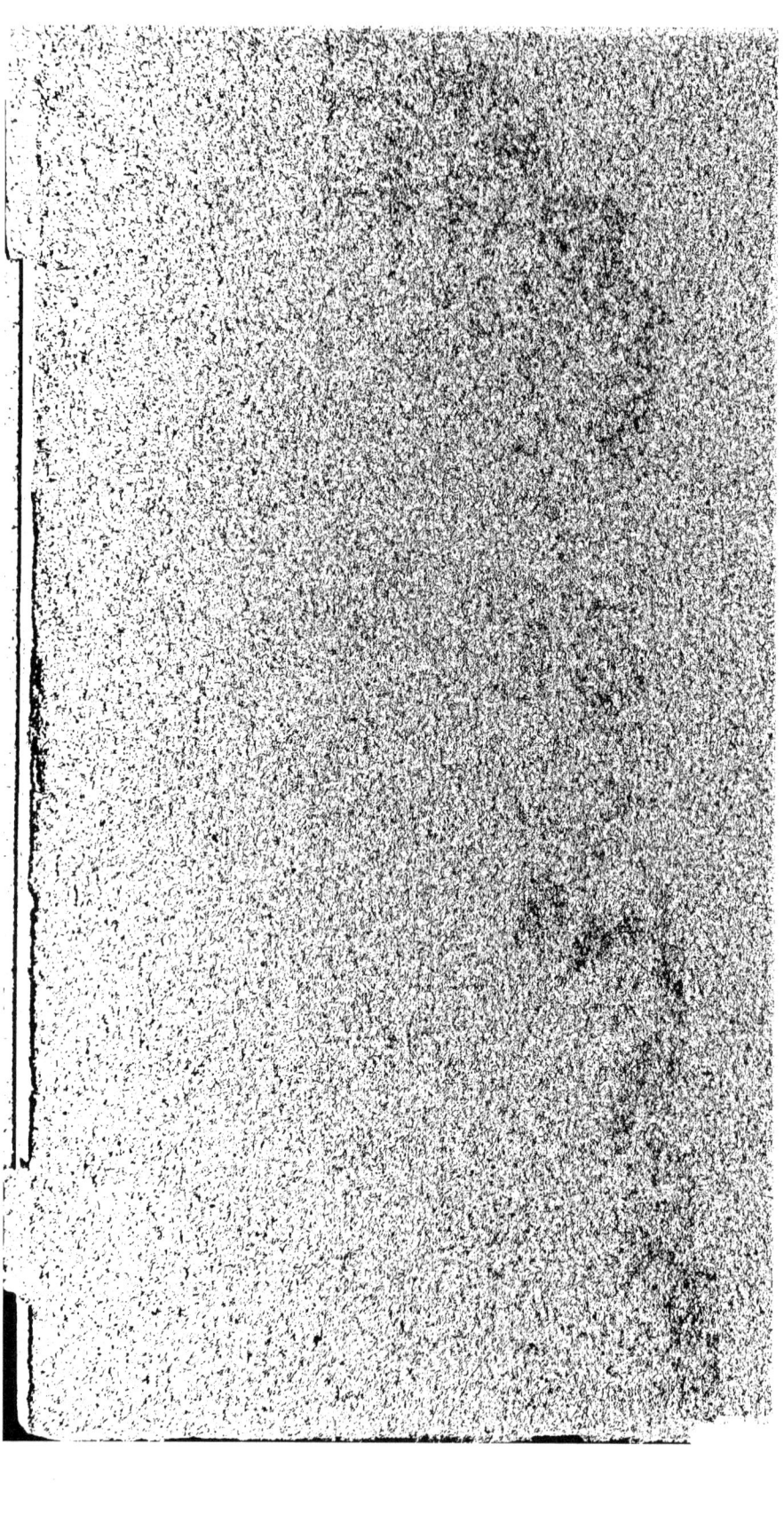

CPSIA information can be obtained
at www.ICGtesting.com
Printed in the USA
BVHW040446261118
533755BV00037B/237/P